PAGE 1 -
Photo: David J. Gubernick
Wild Mustard at Mission Fields, Carmel.

LEFT -
Photo: Rita Costa-Holmann.
A farmhouse stands amidst the productive fields near Spreckels.

RIGHT -
Photo: Gregory Weeks.
The sky glows with a warmth as the sun sets over Soberanes Point.

ISBN 1-930401-04-3

Printed in China
10 9 8 7 6 5 4 3 2

*Front Cover Photograph: Rita Costa-Hollmann. Pacific Grove. Back Cover
Photographs: Left - Gregory Weeks. Hayfields. Right - Gregory Weeks. Big Sur
coast. Copyright Page Photograph: Gregory Weeks. Mouth of Little Sur
River. Quotes from the book* "Steinbeck Country" *used with permission of
Graphic Arts Center Publishing.*

Publisher:

CENTRAL COAST PRESS
P.O. Box 3654
San Luis Obispo, California 93403

CONTENTS

INTRODUCTION

"From the very beginning it was important to me that the book be primarily a visual experience, and therefore it became a book not about Steinbeck but rather about Steinbeck Country—the land in which he grew up, which must have formed him and stimulated him in much the same way that it stimulated me. But where Steinbeck concerned himself mainly with the people of this land and turned his thoughts and his pen to them, my interest lies in the land itself in all its forms and manifestations."

Steve Crouch

Photo: Lucy Ash. Sun filters through a dense overhead canopy.

It has been over a quarter century since Steve Crouch wrote these words in the Afterword to his book *Steinbeck Country* (1973), years that have seen many changes to the area that both John Steinbeck and Steve Crouch loved and immortalized. Foremost among these changes are the rapid growth and expansion of Salinas and the cities of the Monterey Peninsula coupled with increased tourism throughout the entire region. Yet, in some areas of Steinbeck Country, the changes are more subtle and in still others almost non-existent.

Driving on Highway 101 through the Salinas Valley the Santa Lucias are still the dark, forbidding mountains while the Gabilans are the warm, welcoming ones as so vividly described by John Steinbeck in *East of Eden* (1952) and *The Red Pony* (1938).

The Big Sur coast is still pounded by surf with Highway 1 subject to winter washouts. Standing on a narrow flat jutting out into the ocean near Lucia you can still be the last to see the sun set as Joseph Wayne and the old man did in *To a God Unknown* (1933).

Over the years Steinbeck Country has attracted many artists, writers and photographers. Their legacy, as well as the changes that have occurred, are the focus of the text and photographs of *Steinbeck Country Revisited*.

*   *   *

On a more personal note, for the past 16 years I have been leading numerous day trips to Steinbeck Country. Further, my husband and I have been exploring Steinbeck Country both by car and on foot for more than twenty years. These explorations have heightened our appreciation of the strong sense of place that permeates John Steinbeck's writings and that was shared by Steve Crouch both in his writing and his photographs.

Finally I want to thank my husband, Jerry, for his support and helpful suggestions throughout the writing of this book and my daughter, Irene, for her close reading of the text.

PHOTOGRAPHERS' FOREWORD

Photo: David J. Gubernick. After winter departs, the hills of Steinbeck Country are filled with new growth, harbingers of warmer weather to come.

Steve Crouch's *Steinbeck Country* is a local classic that pays homage to the land and people John Steinbeck immortalized in his writings. Our book, *Steinbeck Country Revisited*, was always envisioned first and foremost as a visual, photographic representation of Steinbeck Country and people. The impetus for *Steinbeck Country Revisited* was provided by Rocky Jordon, one of the founding members of the Independent Photographers.

We are a group of professional and serious amateur photographers drawn together by our love of photography and our desire to share and explore separate visions. We share these visions monthly at the Monterey Museum of Art, thanks to the generous support and participation of Richard W. Gadd, Executive Director.

Twenty-seven photographers rose to the challenge of producing a body of work worthy of the heritage provided by Steve Crouch. It was no easy task. Therefore, we selected a committee (Kira Carrillo Corser, Richard W. Gadd, David J. Gubernick) to edit more than 1,000 images; 250 of these were submitted to the publisher. The publisher decided which photographs would appear in the book, and selected a writer to provide accompanying text.

Steinbeck Country Revisited is a group effort that pays humble tribute to Steve Crouch and John Steinbeck by photographically revisiting, almost thirty years after *Steinbeck Country* was published, the land that Steinbeck and Crouch loved.

Independent Photographers

STEINBECK COUNTRY:
A PORTFOLIO

"John Steinbeck writes descriptions so powerful and visceral, so full of earth and so visually oriented–in other words so photographic in their impression..."

Rocky Jordan

Photo: Richard W. Gadd
The old sugar beet factory at Spreckels.

LEFT - Photo: Mary Frost
Cypress trees are synonymous with the
Monterey Coast—they have the ability
to cling tenaciously to life along rocky
cliffs and sandy shores alike.

RIGHT - Photo: Mary Wurtz
Visitors meander outside Monterey's
number one tourist draw—Monterey
Bay Aquarium in Steinbeck's Cannery
Row.

Photo: Rita Costa-Hollmann. While modern technological innovations arrive with increasing frequency, the fishing industry seems a world apart–using traditional methods handed down through generations.

Photo: David Glover. All of Monterey's fish canneries did not disappear in past decades–some continue to thrive on the Pacific's bounty.

ABOVE - Photo: Mary Frost. Evening arrives along the edge of Monterey Bay at Lover's Point, Pacific Grove—a nice place for couples to stroll.

LEFT - Photo: David Glover. The aging foundations of Cannery Row, which once supported the bustling canneries described by John Steinbeck, now carry the weight of booming tourist shops and restaurants.

ABOVE - Photo: David Glover. Relentless in its age-old task, the constant surf wears away at the hardest of rocks. (Garrapata Beach, Big Sur)

LEFT - Photo: Kira Carrillo Corser. A few steps off the main highway in Big Sur and visitors find themselves in a primordial world of damp heavy air and lush green vegetation. (Joshua Creek, Big Sur)

Photo: Gregory Weeks. Misty Forest—Old Coast Road, Big Sur.

LAND AND SEA

Land and Sea

We emerge from the car,
enter a curtain of fog
wrapping the trees,
the ocean below
in its grip.

Only persistent surf
beating on the shore
breaks through the silence.

Land and sea are joined
in this mantle of gray
until suddenly
the sun bursts through
transforming the landscape
into a cornucopia of
*   shapes and colors.*

Photo: Gregory Weeks. Surf at Garrapata
Beach, Big Sur.

ABOVE - Photo: Rita Costa-Hollmann. Each year the hills are renewed with springtime growth of new grasses, buds and wildflowers.
RIGHT - Photo: Rita Costa-Hollmann. Flowers burst forth with color along Pacific Grove's rocky coastline.

ABOVE - Photo: Kira Carrillo Corser. Shooting Star wildflowers.
RIGHT - Photo: Lucy Ash. During the warmer months when the sun pulses and heats the inland valleys, the cool sea marine air is sucked towards the coast where it remains until the land is cool.

Photo: Kira Carrillo Corser. From the Pacific Ocean comes the storms. Moving from the frigid North Pacific towards the coast, the winter storms release their forces upon the land before continuing to the east.

Photo: Leroy Beal. Long after the seasonal rains have receded, water flows out of the Santa Lucias rushing towards the Pacific Ocean. (Mill Creek along the Big Sur coast).

Photo: David J. Gubernick. Like a snake, the Madrone tree sheds its skin—the smooth reddish bark peels in a once-a-year display.

Photo: Anna Rheim. Lichens cover a native oak tree. Lichens are sensitive to harmful gases and seem to thrive away from the smoke and exhaust fumes of cities.

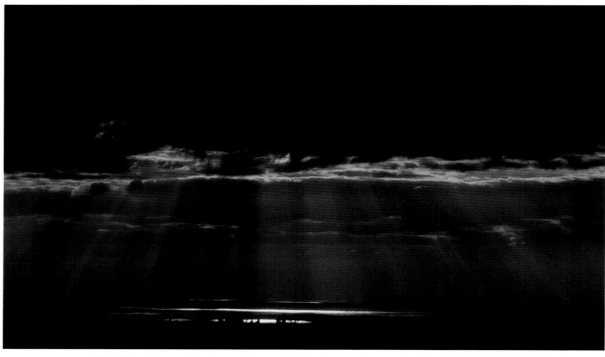

ABOVE - Photo: Marianne Mangold. As the sun descends, the skies are filled with spectacular colors glimmering off the Pacific waters. (Point Lobos)

RIGHT - Photo: Robert Ellis. Muted colors are visible as the fog weaves through outstretched oak branches atop Jack's Peak.

BIG SUR

DUSK IN THE SANTA LUCIAS

Dusk sweeps over the mountain peak
the world below glides
through wispy fog
soft hued rhythmic contours of
hills and valleys
flooded now and then by the sun's
lingering rays.

In the distance
the placid emerald ocean
is torn asunder by sudden swells.
The sun drawn inexorably to the sea
sits momentarily
then slides its perfect golden sphere into
the beckoning depth
until only a faint glow remains.
Loitering clouds transformed
into a crimson herd
streak across the sky
racing toward the night.

Around us dark shadows
flit through the golden grass
bowing in obeisance to the wind.
Your hand in mine
we fade into the twilight.

Photo: David J. Gubernick. Full moon over Big Sur.

BIG SUR

"The region known as the Big Sur lies south of Monterey, stretching along the coast for eighty miles—eighty miles of canyon, precipice, rocky peak, and redwood forest.

This is not gentle country with easy contours. The Sur is a land of steep ups and downs; there is little level ground."

Steve Crouch
Steinbeck Country (1973)

M any changes, both at nature's whim and manmade, have occurred in the Big Sur region since Steve Crouch wrote these words. While there remains some controversy as to the exact southernmost point of the Big Sur region, it is still generally described as stretching from San Simeon in the south to the Carmel area in the north. An estimated 6 million people pass through Big Sur each year. The entire area is known as one of the most spectacular meetings of land and sea in the world. In many places the highway is carved out of the feet of the precipitous western slopes of the Santa Lucia Mountains. Close to 50 streams flow down the mountains to join the sea. The majority of these streams had to be spanned before Highway 1 from San Simeon to Carmel was finally opened to public traffic on June 29, 1937. (One summer, in the early 1920's, John Steinbeck was part of a survey group mapping the northern area of the road.) However, the opening of the road was not and probably never will be the end of slides and washouts during and after winters of drenching rains. From the winding, two-lane road Big Sur looks much as it did when Steve Crouch described it in the early 70s. Ridges plunge thousands of feet into the sea. Cattle graze on verdant headlands. Especially in the southern portion, only a few small communities dot the roadside.

In order to construct Highway 1 from San Simeon to Carmel,

the natural angles of some slopes have been altered, making them less stable. This human surgery inflicted on the landscape is less than perfect and from time to time nature reclaims its own. In some years, heavy winter rains have caused closure of Highway 1 beyond Ragged Point for anywhere from a few weeks to over a year. A landslide, over 1,000 feet high and three times as wide, in the area of Pfeiffer-Burns State Park, as well as several more minor slides, closed the road for 13 months in 1983. In 1998, another year of El Niño, some 40 slides along the entire stretch of the road resulted in a closure of four months.

BIG SUR SLIDE
Like a rattlesnake shedding its skin
rocks slither
        off the side of the mountain
roll ever faster
        down the steep slope
        bound across the highway
rush recklessly toward
        burial in the churning sea.

The seasonal rains hitting the coast are sometimes accompanied by winds of up to 100 miles per hour, with the ability to fracture the highway, fell trees, carry away roofs, trash houses, and wipe out gardens. The slides sometimes cause the isolation of the residents of the coast and take away their tourist income. Yet the majority of them stay and rebuild and cheer each other on.

At the southernmost point of the Big Sur, at San Simeon, the coast is still gentle, the hills rolling. The chief attraction here for the millions of tourists from all over the world arriving in passengers cars, motor homes and tour buses continues to be the white marble palace, Graeco-Roman-Moorish in design, designed by Julia Morgan for William Randolph Hearst. The Castle was established as a State Historical Monument in 1948. In 1987 an

Photo: Bob Brueggeman. Follow the Waterfall Trail to view McWay Falls within Julia Pfeiffer Burns State Park.

ABOVE - Photo: David Glover. The mountains of the Big Sur coast are home to literally hundreds of waterfalls. LEFT - Photo: Kira Carrillo Corser. Plaskett Ridge Road winds its way into the steep inclines of the Santa Lucias, one of the few drivable passages from central Big Sur to the inland valley.

Photo: Gregory Weeks. The Spanish named this river "El Rio Chiquito del Sur" which was shortened in English to the "Little Sur River".

elaborate Visitor Center was built at the foot of the castle. Included in that center is a theater with a five-story screen and seven channel surround sound.

The nearby land is still owned by the Hearst Corporation. Their proposal to build a large resort and golf course at San Simeon has created a certain amount of controversy. Environmentalists and many residents of the region have expressed their concern to the Coastal Commision regarding the effect such a project would have on the ecology, traffic and overall environment of the area.

The beach a few miles north of San Simeon attracts visitors of a different sort. While once not found south of Año Nuevo in Santa Cruz County, these visitors now come here by the thousands to mate, give birth to their young, and to molt. They are Northern Elephant Seals whose populations have increased to the point that they have colonized this sandy beach and made it their own. Monterey Bay Marine Sanctuary docents have noted that at the height of the season up to 5,000 elephant seals can be observed from the viewing point above. On a spring day only several hundred remain. Occasionally they flip sand over their bodies, or slowly move a few feet closer to the surf, before resuming their resting positions.

Beyond San Carpoforo Creek, the Santa Lucia Range crowds the highway, making the road between there and the Ragged Point Inn among the curliest stretches with a sharp drop-off to the restless sea below. The most recent wilderness acquisition by the U.S. Forest Service is the Sur Sur Ranch (formerly known as the Baldwin Ranch), immediately east of the Ragged Point Inn. The ranch, now open to hikers and backpackers, encompasses a land of rolling hills and rugged cliffs, grassy meadows and mountain ridges with spectacular views. In the spring and early summer the area boasts a profusion of wildflowers and rushing creeks.

South of the tiny community of Lucia one side of the high-

Photo: Robert Ellis. Algae, leaf and grass.

way is often washed out. John Steinbeck must have known the Lucia area well, for it is surely the area he describes towards the end of *To a God Unknown* (1933). Steinbeck relates how in a year of severe drought Joseph Wayne and his brother, Thomas, ride from the parched San Antonio River Valley west of Jolon over the Santa Lucia Mountains to the coast. Along the way they hear the tinkle of a bell and then meet an old man who invites them to his house on "a long narrow flat." Near the house, at the cliff's edge, the old man had built a platform to observe the sunset. He is convinced that from there he is "the last man in the western world" to see the sun set. The Lucia Lodge, long operated by members of the pioneer Harlan family, is very likely the location of the fictional house and platform.

Photo: Kira Carrillo Corser. Nature encroaches upon this old cabin which begins its descent into decay.

Photo: Rita Costa-Hollmann. Andrew Molera State Park was named after Andrew Molera, great grandson of John Cooper who was one of the first settlers in Big Sur.

Photo: Gregory Weeks. An old log bridge, deteriorated after decades of neglect.

The prime distinguishing factors of the area of the Big Sur coast have been its relative isolation, sparse settlement and spectacular beauty. These factors make it an excellent research and study area for biologists and ecologists, as well as presenting the opportunity to preserve large areas for future generations. Foremost among these areas, a few miles north of Lucia, is the 4,000 acre Big Creek Ranch. It was acquired by the Nature Conservancy in 1977 and subsequently transferred to the University of California to become part of the UC Natural Land and Water Reserves System. In 1978 it was renamed the Landels-Hill Big Creek Reserve. The area extends from sea level to an elevation of about 3,500 feet and includes areas of redwood, pine and mixed hardwood forest, open grassland and scrub communities. Since the arrival of the first white settlers in the 1800's, the land has remained in a semi-wilderness condition. This makes it a prime study and research area, drawing both undergraduate and graduate student researchers from UC campuses and other institutions. Close to two hundred species of terrestrial vertebrates have been identified. Although the area is closed to the public, the Nature Conservancy provides occasional public guided tours.

In January 1994, the California Fish and Game Administration established the Big Creek Marine Ecological Reserve. The boundary of the reserve encompasses about 3 1/2 miles of shoreline and extends one mile offshore. Here fishes and other marine organisms are protected from harvesting, allowing many species to grow and reach their full reproductive potential, thus benefiting over-harvested populations. The Reserve is contiguous with the Landels-Hill Big Creek Reserve and is co-administered by the California Department of Fish and Game and the University of California at Santa Cruz.

While the drive along the Big Sur Coast presents an unending panorama of breathtaking vistas, the best way to fully experience this unique gift of nature is on foot. The many beaches, some sandy, others rocky lure the beachcomber in search of pebbles and shells. Or, perhaps, you will want to explore the world of the many tide pools, or just sit and let the music of the waves renew your energy. Another time, walking along the beach, you might be startled to see a dead seal surrounded by a circle of vultures. John Steinbeck was familiar with this area and perhaps a similar experience was the genesis for his graphic description of Jody's encounter with these raptors in *The Red Pony* (1938).

The spectacular beauty of the Big Sur coast has long attracted writers, artists, musicians and crafts people in search of both solitude and inspiration. Among these was Henry Miller, who made his home on Partington Ridge from 1944 to 1962. During Miller's time in Big Sur, people in large numbers made pilgrimages to visit the great "underground" writer whose works had been banned in the United States. One of these was Miller's friend, writer and artist Emil White, who not only visited, but stayed. One of the books Miller wrote while living on Partington Ridge was *Big Sur and the Oranges of Hieronymus Bosch* (1957). He dedicated the book to Emil, writing that Emil was one of the few friends who had never failed him. Miller died in Pacific Palisades in 1980. In 1981 Emil White donated his property in Graves Canyon to the Big Sur Land Trust (founded in 1978) and with their assistance converted his Graves Canyon home into the Henry Miller Library. It was his tribute to his friend and for the next eight years he welcomed and chatted with young and old visitors from all over the world. The Library, with its extensive collection of Miller books, photos, videos and memorabilia, lies in a peaceful grove flanked by a lush meadow surrounded by venerable, towering redwoods. Since Emil White's death in 1989, the Big Sur Land Trust has been caring for the library. It is open to the public and, under the directorship of Magnus Toren, has evolved into a community center for Big Sur artists, poets and writers. The library has sponsored a symposium on Robinson Jeffers, weekly poetry readings and other special events. It also publishes the journal "Ping Pong" carrying reviews of Miller's publications and art as

well as essays on the culture and art, both past and present, of Big Sur.

Bob Nash was one of the many artists who came to Big Sur. He arrived in 1951 as just another refugee of the Beat Generation. Unlike many others, he persevered and stayed and is today recognized as one of Big Sur's outstanding artists. Some of his over 26,000 non-objective line drawings are housed in the permanent collection of the Monterey Peninsula Museum of Art and the Henry Miller Library. They have also been exhibited all over the world. In 1996 the Henry Miller Library, with the financial help of Nash's many friends and admirers, published Bob Nash's book, *On My Way: fragments of my life as an artist.* Looking back at his life from his home on Partington Ridge, Nash reflects upon his growth as an artist. He reveals the influences that shaped his unique artistic style — the chaotic beauty of nature, the simplicity of haiku, the joys of his discoveries, his friendships with Edward Weston and Henry Miller and his life in Big Sur. The limited edition book includes a selection of his drawings.

One of the most vivid and powerful descriptions of the terrain in the Santa Lucia mountains occurs in John Steinbeck's short story "Flight." Those mountains have changed little since the story was written in the 1930's. Pepe's flight on horseback and later on foot across the mountains is so graphically portrayed that an intrepid rider or hiker today might well be able to follow Pepe's route through canyons, stream beds, up and down steep trails, ridges and dry slopes. The landscape is such that he might even imagine he sees "one of the dark watchers" on a distant ridge.

Since the passage of the California Coastal Conservation Act by voters in 1976, various proposals for the Big Sur coast have been debated. These include making Highway 1 into a toll road, and turning Big Sur into a National Park. However, since these proposals elicited controversy both among local residents and politicians, none were passed. The most populated part of the Big Sur, the area north of the Henry Miller Library, has seen the most changes. The changes include the construction of two high-priced resorts (Ventana Inn and Post Ranch Inn) as well as some large, expensive houses. Fortunately none of these obstruct the views from the highway. At the same time the Big Sur Land Trust has worked hard to acquire and protect some of the most scenic lands in the area.

The descendants of many of the original settlers in Big Sur still live and make their living there. Most of the Beats and hippies of the 1950's, 1960's and early 1970's no longer roam the land, yet it is still an area that attracts not only the millions of tourists, but also men and women who come seeking a simpler life away from the rush of the cities.

The Bixby Creek Bridge, located approximately half way between the village of Big Sur and Carmel, is one of the world's highest single-span concrete arch bridges. Reaching over 260 feet high and over 700 feet long, it is a structural masterpiece renowned for its beauty.

Since 1986 the Big Sur International Marathon, visually one of the most breathtaking marathons in the country, has been a yearly late April occurrence. It started as an event for runners in Monterey County and is still limited to 3,000 runners. Over the years it has achieved an international reputation, attracting participants from all over the world. Some 1,800 volunteers work to make the event a success, with proceeds going directly to local non-profits. During the Sunday happening the road is closed to traffic. The 26.2 mile route runs south to north from Pfeiffer Big Sur State Park to the Carmel River Bridge. In addition to the marathon, the day now includes a five-person relay, a 5-K run and 7-, 10- and 21-mile walks, bringing the total number of participants up to 8,000. An estimated 25,000 spectators cheer the participants on and applaud them on their return.

The Runner

He runs past the finish line
vibrating bones grinding
pulsing muscles flexing
bald skull glistening
ecstatic pain flooding his face.

Photo: Heidi McGurrin. Bixby Bridge, built
in the 1930's, was one of the longest single
span bridges of its time. In the photograph,
marathon runners from around the world
cross the bridge.

Photo: Anna Rheim. The Point Sur Lighthouse, built in 1899, sits on a step-sided sandstone island connected to the mainland by a sandy causeway.

LEFT - Photo: Heidi McGurrin. The gentler slopes of the Santa Lucias are awash in color as spring wildflowers adorn the Big Sur coast.

RIGHT - Photo: Mary Wurtz. Belltower of Mission San Carlos Borromeo del Rio Carmelo.

CARMEL

CARMEL

I n December of 1602 the explorer Vizcaíno named the Carmel River in honor of the Carmelite priests accompanying him. Carmel Bay, Carmel Mission and the City of Carmel (originally called Carmel-by-the-Sea) all derive from Vizcaíno's original naming. The City of Carmel, although not incorporated until 1916, to a great extent got its start as an indirect result of the 1906 San Francisco earthquake for it became a retreat and refuge for writers, artists and free thinkers displaced by that earthquake. Among these were Mary Austin, Jack London, George Sterling and Upton Sinclair, to name just a few. In more recent years, renowned photographic artists Ansel Adams, Edward Weston and Cole Weston made their homes in Carmel.

Ansel Adams (1902-1984) and Edward Weston (1896-1958) were both among the founders of the f/64 group in 1932. The group chose that optical term because they habitually set their lenses to that aperture to secure maximum image sharpness to both foreground and distance. Both Adams and Weston photographed some of the same California landscape, yet their approach was different. In his introduction to *The Portfolios of Ansel Adams* (1981) John Szarkowski commented that Adams' landscapes are "based on the translation of light into precise tonal relationships" while "the landscape in Weston's pictures is seen as sculpture: round, weighty and fleshily sensuous."

The work of both men is exhibited in Carmel at the Weston Gallery founded in 1976 by Margaret Weston. For thirty years after his father's death in 1958, Cole Weston continued making prints of his father's negatives stamped "Negative by Edward Weston, Print by Cole Weston." Since 1988, he has devoted his time to his own color photography, with subjects ranging from landscapes and nudes, to weathered buildings and industrial ruins. Now in his 70s, Cole Weston still lives in Monterey County.

Photographic art is still very much a part of Carmel today. In 1988, The Center for Photographic Art was established as a non-profit Public Benefit Corporation for the purpose of encouraging increased awareness and understanding of photography as a fine art form.

At the time of the incorporation of Carmel, the residents voted against sidewalks and streetlights in the residential district and that is how the area remains. Although the streets are named, there are no numbers on the houses and, as a result, residents still need to pick up their mail at the post office. While many of the houses are old and small, those few that are for sale are beyond the budget of the average buyer.

According to long-time Carmel resident, community activist and historian, Marjory Lloyd, interviewed by me a few years before her death in 1992, these inflated housing prices, affordable only to the well-to-do, represent quite a change from the 1930's when most of the residents could barely make ends meet. She recalled the parties at Jack Calvin's house on Mission Street that she and her husband attended together with John and Carol Steinbeck, Ed Ricketts, and a number of their other financially strapped friends. They shared meals, stories and friendship and sometimes a bottle of cheap wine. She was sad that, years later, when Steinbeck returned to California on his trip researching his book, *Travels with Charley* (1962), he did not contact her and some of his other old friends as he did not want to see "what had happened to them."

Francis Whitaker, the artist blacksmith whose work made the name "The Forge in the Forest" well known in Carmel, was one of the group of friends that had met at Jack Calvin's house as well as Ricketts' Lab in Monterey. In 1996 a large group of Whitaker's friends, among them his daughter, Sheila, feted him

RIGHT - Photo: Steve G. Shapiro. The Carmel River looking to the east towards Carmel Valley.

ABOVE - Photo: Mary Wurtz. Carmel is sometimes described as a town of fairytale architecture.

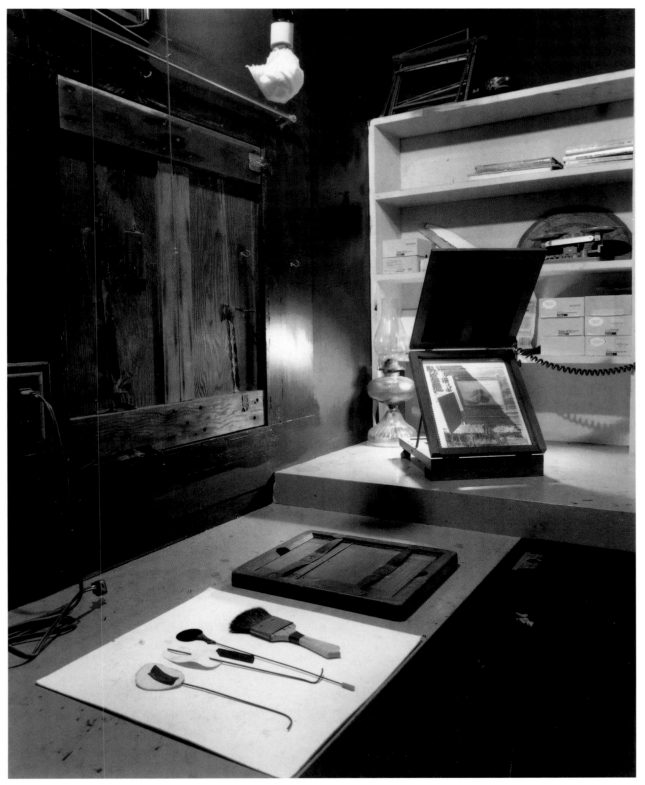

Photo: Robert Almeida. The darkroom of local photographer Edward Weston (1902-1958) is preserved.

Whitaker passed away in October of 1997 in Colorado.

One of the most famous sites in Carmel is renowned poet Robinson Jeffers' (1887-1962) Tor House on a point of land that meets the sea. Robinson and his wife Una came to Carmel in search of a wild coast where he could write in seclusion. They called the point where they built their house, The Tor, after the coast in Devon, England it resembled. Their twin boys Garth and Donnan grew up at Tor House and in 1993 Yolla Bolly Press published both sons' Tor House memories. Garth died in the summer of 1998 more than a decade after his brother. Since 1978, Tor House and adjacent Hawk Tower, built by Robinson for Una, has been maintained by The Robinson Jeffers Tor House Foundation, a non-profit organization. The volunteer members conduct tours and sponsor an Annual Jeffers Festival in October.

The rebuilding of the Carmel Mission, begun in 1931, was finally completed in 1981. The Mission had been founded by Junípero Serra in 1771 and his remains are in the Basilica next to his friend Padre Juan Crespí. The Mission attracts visitors from all over the world, the most notable being Pope John Paul II, who visited in 1987 as part of his tour of the United States.

While the City of Carmel now has a population of only about 4,500 in its approximate square mile core, the business district with its studios, galleries, antique stores, boutiques, small cafes and restaurants is crowded every day with tourists of all ages from all over the world. In addition to viewing the galleries and studios, visitors come to attend the numerous festivals aimed at promoting and enhancing the creative tradition of Carmel. Among others, these include the Carmel Art Festival, Art Walk, Bach Festival and Shakespeare Festival. As a result, parking spaces are at a premium and often bumper to bumper traffic crawls along Highway 1 in the Carmel area as well as on Ocean Avenue in Carmel.

Photo: Gale Wrausmann. Artist at work along Carmel Beach.

on his 90th birthday. The celebration was at the restored First Murphy House, now a town community center. Over the fireplace hung a large photograph of Francis striking hot metal on his anvil. Andirons fashioned from pieces of old railroad track, an original Whitaker design, decorated the mantel. A collection of his black and white photographs depicting scenes from in and around Carmel adorned the walls. Francis

Photo: Steve G. Shapiro. Robinson Jeffers' Hawk Tower in Carmel was built by the poet as an act of love for his wife Una. Hawk Tower and Tor House are open to the public on a limited basis.

LEFT - Photo: Robert Ellis. Mission San Carlos Borromeo del Rio Carmelo was founded by Fray Junípero Serra in 1770 in Monterey. It was moved to its present Carmel location near the mouth of the Carmel River in 1771.

RIGHT - Photo: Robert Ellis. An interior view of the Carmelite Monastery located south of Carmel proper opposite Monastery Beach.

Located at the southern point of Carmel Bay, Point Lobos is a mosaic of bold headlands, irregular coves and rolling meadows fashioned over a million years through interaction between land and sea. The Monterey cypress and the Monterey pine are both native to the area. With the help of the Save-the-Redwoods League, Point Lobos passed into the trusteeship of the State of California in 1933 and became known as Point Lobos State Reserve. Deriving its name from the offshore rocks at Punta de los Lobos Marinos, Point of the Sea Wolves, where the sound of the sea lions carries inland, the reserve has often been called "the crown jewel of the State Park System."

Point Lobos was a special place for John Steinbeck and his sister, Mary. As children on family outings, long before it became a State Reserve, they had often spent time there. After Steinbeck's death in New York in December 1968, his

Photo: Leroy Beal. Tile work at Carmel Mission.

wife Elaine and his son Thom brought his ashes to California. In *The True Adventures of John Steinbeck, Writer* (1984), Jackson Benson relates that after the silver box containing John's ashes had rested for two days in the garden of the Eleventh Street house in Pacific Grove, John's sisters arranged for a small service for the family "on Point Lobos, on a cliff overlooking Whalers Bay, a spot that John and Mary had loved and where they had played as children."

Among Point Lobos' dozen short trails, probably the most popular is the Cypress Grove Trail, which winds through one of the two naturally growing stands of Monterey cypress trees remaining on earth. (The other grove is across Carmel Bay at Cypress Point.) Point Lobos was originally acquired to protect these trees. As you hike along the trails and look out at Carmel Bay, you may see egrets and gulls landing on kelp beds close to shore, while sea otters on their backs drift through the floating brown seaweed and harbor seals bask on the rocks. The area is a photographer's paradise. Outstanding among these are Edward Weston's resplendent photographs of the cypress, tidepools and rocks of Point Lobos.

Park authorities call Point Lobos a living museum of land and sea life. In 1960, 750 underwater acres were added to Point Lobos State Reserve, creating the first Marine Reserve in the United States. Since 1973, when it was further designated an Ecological Reserve, intertidal and subtidal plant and animal species have received full protection. In 1992, the Reserve became part of the Monterey Bay National Marine

Photo: Robert Ellis. A well-protected statue at the mission.

Photo: Rita Costa-Hollmann. Carmel Beach stretching from Pebble Beach in the north to Carmel Point in the south, was the site of abalone picnics led by poet George Sterling.

Sanctuary, the nation's largest marine sanctuary. Part of the underwater reserve in Whalers and Bluefish Coves is open to registered scuba divers. In the subdued light of the 70-foot-high kelp forest they enter a world of vibrant color created by animals without backbones and plants without roots. At times they may even find themselves in the company of curious otters and sea lions.

The Whalers Cabin at Whalers Cove was built by Chi-nese fishermen in the 1850s. It was occupied and used from 1851 to 1983 by various families, workers, and in later years, by park personnel. After the last of the occupants moved out in 1983, it was transformed into the Whalers Cabin Museum, a cultural history museum. The adjacent Whaling Station Museum was opened in 1994. Both are staffed by volunteers from the non-profit Point Lobos Natural History Association, formed in 1978.

ABOVE - Photo: Gregory Weeks. Point Lobos is a mosaic of bold headlands, irregular coves and rolling meadows.

RIGHT - Photo: Gregory Weeks. Glorious sunset at Carmel Point.

WHALERS COVE

Fingers of fog
  slide over the shore
wind blown surf
  sprays sea sculptured rock.
The incoming tide surges,
  spills over a time bleached log
before reluctantly
  retreating.

ABOVE - Photo: Kira Carrillo Corser. Whaler's cabin at Point Lobos.

CARMEL VALLEY

T he Carmel River winds its way from the Santa Lucia Mountains through the Carmel Valley to Carmel Bay. In Steinbeck's *Cannery Row* (1945), when Mack and the boys drive in the old Model T to the river to look for frogs for Doc, Steinbeck refers to it as "a lovely little river." It is still a lovely little river today, although it is threatened by sedimentation.

The Spanish explorer Sebastian Viscaíno discovered and named the Carmel River and the Carmel Valley in 1602. Large cattle ranches were established during the land grant era, to be followed in the 20th century by dairy farms and fruit orchards. The nature of the area began to change in 1969 when Carmel Valley's first major commercial vineyard was planted in the Cachagua region of the valley by Bill Durney. Since then, a number of other vineyards have sprung up in the valley. The unincorporated community of Carmel Valley Village now features at least five wine-tasting rooms drawing large numbers of visitors. As a result, the village is rapidly becoming a destination location.

Fortunately, since the 1972 creation of the Monterey Peninsula Regional Park District, there has also been an attempt to preserve existing open spaces. The District's first acquisition, in December of 1975, was the 541-acre William M. Garland Ranch, a few miles outside of Carmel Valley Village. Through gifts and purchase additions, Garland Regional Park now encompasses 4,462 acres. Much of what makes up Garland Park today was part of the Meadows Mexican Land Grant, subsequently owned by Samuel F. B. Morse of the Pacific Improvement Co. (Del Monte Properties). The Park contains a wide range of terrain and vegetation. It extends from the 200-foot elevation of the willow-covered banks of the Carmel River up to 2,000 feet in the Santa Lucia Mountains, where it offers spectacular vistas. Equestrian, biking and hiking trails throughout the park give the visitor an opportunity

Photo: David J. Gubernick. Carmel Valley contains a mix of ranchlands, farms and untouched wilderness.

not only to view a diversity of vegetation and wildlife, but to step back in time and view Rumsien Indian habitation sites; homestead, hunting and logging remains; livestock trails, ponds and springs.

Hidden Valley, an institute of the Performing Arts, moved its location from Monterey to a 10-acre site a few miles east of Garland Regional Park in 1972. The Institute had its origins in Southern California and was named for its first site in

ABOVE - Photo: David J. Gubernick. Rapidly expanding vineyards of Carmel Valley produce fine California wines.
PAGE 58 LEFT - Photo: David J. Gubernick. Big sky in Carmel Valley.

ABOVE - Photo: David J. Gubernick. Wild Mule Deer roam freely throughout the golden hills of the California Central Coast.

RIGHT - Photo: David J. Gubernick. An oak tree stands sentinel over a green Carmel Valley.

RIGHT - Photo: Robert Ellis. Spring wildflowers dot the slopes of the Laureles Grade which runs between Carmel Valley and Highway 68.
LEFT - Photo: Robert Almeida. Arroyo Seco, or "dry creek" lies at the eastern end of Carmel Valley and heads inland to the Salinas Valley

the Angeles National Forest. Located in the midst of Steinbeck country, in addition to being a training center "providing young talents from around the world with performance and study opportunities", it hosts numerous Elderhostel programs including a class devoted to John Steinbeck. (Elderhostels are worldwide residential educational programs for ages 55 and up.)

Highway G16 winds from Hidden Valley to Greenfield, changing its name from Carmel Valley Road to Arroyo Seco Road. Traffic here is much lighter for there are no large developments, only a few scattered clusters of mailboxes along the road indicating homes or ranches nearby. In former years between miles 26 and 27, several signs nailed on trees by the side of the road asked passing drivers to "please avoid newts crossing road." However, on several recent drives, no newts were seen there or anywhere

along the road. You might instead need to brake for a family of quail crossing the road or, if you are driving in the early morning or around dusk, a doe with her fawn. In the spring, after the heavy winter rains, a profusion of lupines and poppies lend a festive air to both sides of the road and groves of cottonwoods show off their finery.

She leans into spring
drunk on its heady perfume.
Wind feeds her frenzy.

PACIFIC GROVE

Ever since World War II change has been ongoing—change in the way we live, where we live and how we live. Yet, there are still some communities that have only been lightly touched by the incessant flow toward change. Pacific Grove, with its over one thousand Victorian homes and cottages, hailed as "The Last Hometown," is one of these communities. Pacific Grove begins at the Monterey Bay Aquarium and ends at the 17 Mile Drive Gate.

On a summer day, when next door Monterey is crowded with tourists, only a few history buffs walk the streets of Pacific Grove. Most likely they are looking for the houses where Ed Ricketts had his first lab and lived and where John Steinbeck lived and wrote several of his early books including *The Pastures of Heaven* (1932), immortalizing some of the areas he knew so well. (El Corral de Tierra, the actual location for *The Pastures of Heaven* (1932), with the exception of a few large new homes, has seen little change over the years.) Today Ed Ricketts' home, the Steinbeck family cottage, John Steinbeck's cottage and Elizabeth Hamilton's cottage are all private residences.

Elizabeth Hamilton was Steinbeck's maternal grandmother. Richard Andolsen, the current owner of the Elizabeth Hamilton cottage, is a great admirer of the works of John Steinbeck. He welcomes visitors and enjoys telling them about and showing them the small workroom attached to the main house that Steinbeck and his brother-in-law built in 1936. He also urges visitors to join his campaign to have Stanford University (Steinbeck's alma mater) create a Steinbeck fellowship.

The work of John Steinbeck's close friend, marine biologist Ed Ricketts, has inspired several generations of biologists. In 1994, the City of Pacific Grove renamed High Street "Ricketts Row." In 1997, a plaque was placed at the corner of Ricketts Row and Fountain Avenue to mark the site of Ricketts' first lab.

Unlike so many other communities, the downtown business section of Pacific Grove is alive and flourishing. Holman's Department Store, the site of the flagpole skater in *Cannery Row* (1945), has been refurbished and now is primarily devoted to antiques and collectibles. Many other stores, restaurants, coffee shops, gift shops and galleries as well as the excellent Pacific Grove Museum of Natural History are located in the downtown area.

As a young boy Steinbeck spent many summers and weekends with his family in Pacific Grove. Jackson Benson in *The True Adventures of John Steinbeck, Writer* (1984) states that the family and their friends went for hikes "along the water and into the nearby hills around Asilomar." Since John Steinbeck was born in 1902, those hikes were probably before the 105 acres of forest, dunes and beach at the southwestern edge of Pacific Grove became a camp and conference center for the YWCA in 1913. Julia Morgan, commissioned by Phoebe Apperson Hearst (the mother of William Randolph Hearst), was the architect of many of the Arts and Crafts-style buildings constructed at Asilomar between 1913

Photo: David J. Gubernick. Point Piños Lighthouse was founded in 1855 in Pacific Grove.

and 1928. Morgan built with the awareness that "nature was something to be lived in, not conquered" and designed the buildings to fit into and grow out of their surroundings, a task she accomplished.

Since 1956 Asilomar (meaning "refuge by the sea") has

PAGE 64-65: LEFT - Photo: Rita Costa-Hollmann. Ice plants along the Pacific Grove coast. RIGHT - Photo: Mary Wurtz. Welcome sign.

Butterfly Trees

For days on end
clusters of Monarchs
garlanding the trees
spread their wings,
spiral gracefully
in step with
the shifting sun.

TOP - Photo: Lucy Ash. Monarch Butterfly. BOTTOM - Photo: Kira Carrillo Corser. Monarch Butterfly caterpillar. Pacific Grove is home to the Monarch Butterfly migration—they cluster by the thousands in the local pine and eucalyptus trees.

TOP - Photo: Lucy Ash. Annual Butterfly Parade in Pacific Grove.
BOTTOM - Photo: Steve Shapiro. Rustic gates at a Pebble Beach home.

been operated by the State of California. Its official name is Asilomar State Beach and Conference Grounds. As of the summer of 1997, a concessionaire, the Delaware North Park Services, operates the lodging and conference business at Asilomar and it is now available for private reservations as well as for groups. In recent years, writers' groups and workshops have been among the many different groups holding their conferences at Asilomar. Perhaps during their stay there among the pines and coast live oaks that John Steinbeck knew and loved, his spirit and legacy have served as inspiration for their members' writings.

In Chapter 38 of *Sweet Thursday* (1954), entitled "Hooptedoole (2), or the Pacific Grove Butterfly Festival," John Steinbeck writes about the plight of the town of Pacific Grove the year the Monarch butterflies did not arrive. In 1954 he was gently poking fun at the citizens of Pacific Grove and their festival. In the years since then, beginning each October, thousands of Monarch butterflies have been clustering together on pines and eucalyptus trees primarily in the Monarch Grove Sanctuary and Washington Park in Pacific Grove. Pacific Grove still holds its annual Butterfly Parade in October. However, today, the phenomenon of the annual Monarch migration is endangered by the constant pressures of coastal development and dwindling open space.

TOP - Photo: Gale Wrausmann. Sunset beyond Pebble Beach's 17 Mile Drive.
BOTTOM - Photo: Rita Costa-Hollman. Pebble Beach is known for its scenic golf courses of unsurpassed beauty.

MONTEREY

LEFT - Photo: Mary Wurtz. Old cannery buildings have been converted to cater to tourists.

RIGHT - Photo: Rita Costa-Hollman. The pelican , once threatened, is now a familiar site throughout the Central Coast.

BELOW LEFT - Photo: Rita Costa-Hollmann. The beach along Cannery Row, formerly the site of noisy canneries, now houses restaurants and shops.

BELOW RIGHT - Photo: Gregory Weeks. Full moon over Cannery Row.

MONTEREY

I n 1902, when John Steinbeck was born, his hometown of Salinas and the City of Monterey each had a population of around 3,000. Unlike the rapid growth of Salinas, the population of the City of Monterey has increased far less. However, that does not count the millions of tourists that visit Monterey the year around. While the attractions are many and varied, ranging from Fisherman's Wharf and "The Path of History Walking Tour" in historic Old Monterey, to Cannery Row (originally called Ocean Avenue), probably the prime attraction for the millions of visitors yearly is the Monterey Bay Aquarium at the northwestern end of Cannery Row.

Fisherman's Wharf, once the center of commercial fishing activity, is today a tourist attraction featuring an art gallery, gift shops, restaurants, sightseeing and fishing cruises. However, standing at the edge of the pier overlooking Monterey Bay, with the fresh wind whipping your hair, you can still be captivated by the antics of surfacing seals and sea otters, the colorful sails of small boats and the rhythmic swells of the ocean. Or, if you have read Steinbeck's *The Log from the Sea of Cortez* (1951), you might try to picture the crowd of friends that came to see Ed Ricketts and John Steinbeck setting off in the *Western Flyer* on their 1940 collecting expedition to the Gulf of California. Anthony John "Tony" Berry, the skipper and last surviving member of that voyage died in 1998 at the age of 92. In *The Log from the Sea of Cortez,* Steinbeck described him as a "good master" who

ABOVE - Photo: Rita Costa-Hollmann. Fisherman's Wharf remains a working wharf as well as a popular tourist destination.

LEFT - Photo: Rita Costa-Hollmann. Some areas of Cannery Row have remained relatively unchanged for decades.

ABOVE - Photo: Richard W. Gadd. Boxes at Monterey Fish Company.

LEFT - Photo: Helene Constant. The fishing industry survives despite having to cope with ever-changing fishing regulations.

ABOVE - Photo: Rita Costa-Hollmann. Views of Fisherman's Wharf, containing restaurants and gift shops as well as a commerical fishing fleet. BOTTOM - Photo: Bob Brueggeman. A fishing boat floats silently in the fog.

LEFT - Photo: David Glover. Steinbeck wrote of "...dirty boats and the clean painted boats..." each one stamped with the personality of the owner. "The Log from the Sea of Cortez."

TOP RIGHT - Photo: Rita Costa-Hollmann. A harbor seal relaxes in the afternoon sun.

BOTTOM RIGHT - Photo: Lucy Ash. Sea creatures such as this Bat Star are abundant throughout the Monterey coast.

guage Center and continues to play a critical role on the Monterey Peninsula as "the cornerstone of the language capital of the world." The Presidio is also active in the environmental restoration and conversion of the former Fort Ord.

The Monterey Bay Aquarium was built on the site of the old Hovden Cannery. Opened in 1984 and enlarged since, the more than 100 galleries and exhibits recreate Monterey Bay's many habitats from shallow tide pools to the vast open ocean. Among its many attractions are a three story kelp forest, the Outer Bay Gallery, and the largest collection of jellyfish in the nation.

The non-profit Monterey Bay Aquarium Research Institute (MBARI), headquartered in Moss Landing, is the Aquarium's sister institution. The Research Institute was founded in 1987 by David Packard (1912-1996) with a mission "to achieve and maintain a position as a world center for advanced research and education in ocean science and technology, through the development of better instruments, systems and methods for scientific research in the deep waters of the ocean." Today it is funded by the Lucile and David Packard Foundation, operates four research vessels, is involved in numerous research studies and in collaboration with the Monterey Bay Aquarium develops creative educational programs.

Photo: Rita Costa-Hollmann. A small boat on Monterey Bay.

"took no chances he could avoid for his boat and his life and ours were no light things for him to tamper with."

Among the many historic Monterey buildings included in "The Path of History Walking Tour" is the Lara-Soto Adobe, where John Steinbeck lived for a short time with Gwyn, his second wife. The Presidio of Monterey lies between old Monterey and Cannery Row. Dating back to before California statehood, it is today home to the Defense Language Institute Foreign Lan-

Photo: Judy Larimore. Salmon ready for the market.

Photo: Rita Costa-Hollmann. Fishermen repairing nets.

The Cannery Row Foundation operates a Visitor Center and small museum in an old railroad car on the Monterey Peninsula Recreation Trail (a former Southern Pacific Railroad right-of-way). The Foundation's mission is "to preserve the sites significant to the historical and literary heritage of Cannery Row and to research and interpret, educate and celebrate the unique multicultural essence of the Cannery Row community." The Foundation sponsors and co-sponsors numerous events including fo-

Photo: Rita Costa-Hollmann. Fishing nets.

rums, tours, and, on February 27 of each year, a John Steinbeck Birthday Celebration. To commemorate Ed Ricketts' contributions to modern marine biology, Cannery Row history, and the literature of John Steinbeck, the Foundation commissioned Pacific Grove sculptor and artist, Jesse Corsaut, to create a life-size bronze memorial of Ed Ricketts. In 1997, on the 100th anniversary of his birth, the memorial, having been funded with the help of donors, was placed at the site where in 1948 Ricketts, attempting to drive his noisy old Packard across the railroad tracks, was struck

Photo: Pat Hathaway. Fish harvest.

by the Del Monte Express. Three days later he died of the injuries he had sustained.

In 1998 the National Trust for Historic Preservation named Cannery Row one of the 11 most endangered historic places in the nation. While the designation contains no legal teeth, it may help to stem the tide of further demolition of existing buildings and proposed new developments, foremost among which is the Cannery Row Marketplace.

A walk along Cannery Row, immortalized in John Steinbeck's *Cannery Row* (1945) and *Sweet Thursday* (1954)

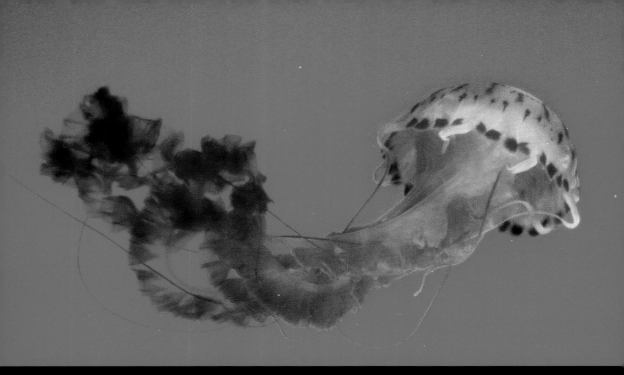

yearly Monterey Jazz Festival.

The conditional ownership of the lab obtained by the City of Monterey in 1994 allowed the club to continue using the building for its activities. In 2004 the city's ownership will be final and the plans are to then turn the lab into a museum featuring exhibits interpreting Ricketts' holistic view of nature, his philosophy, his relationship with John Steinbeck, and his work as collector, author, and biologist. Until that time, the lab is open for public tours twice a year.

To the south of the lab, on both sides of Cannery Row, the City of Monterey Cultural Arts Commission has sponsored the New Cannery Row Mural to camouflage an undeveloped hotel

Photo: Judy Larimore. At the Aquarium, visitors are able to view underwater tanks.

and the site of marine biologist Ed Ricketts' lab, is both a walk through the pages of history and a walk among the tourist consumer society of today. John Steinbeck might have been amused by the fact that in 1991 the bronze bust of him that had stood in the Steinbeck Plaza in the heart of Cannery Row for more than twenty years was stolen. (It was replaced in 1994 with a new bust located on a better, stronger base.) The old canneries have been converted to galleries, boutiques, curio shops, ice cream parlors, and restaurants. There is a Steinbeck Jewelers, Steinbeck Lady, Steinbeck's Espresso Bar, and Steinbeck's Spirit of Monterey Wax Museum all taking advantage of the name of the man who made the Row famous. Yet, just beyond these, at 800 Cannery Row is the historic Ed Ricketts' lab. From 1950 to 1994 it was a private men's social club. That group of men was instrumental in the genesis of the now

Photo: Pat Hathaway. Artist Jay Campbell poses in front of one of the many murals which line Cannery Row.

Photos: Mary Wurtz. Murals along Cannery Row.

Photo: John McCleary. Marine biologist Ed Ricketts' lab is located at 800 Cannery Row. Ed Ricketts was a friend of Steinbeck. Doc Ricketts was a character in the novels "Cannery Row" and "Sweet Thursday."

project site. Monterey artist, author and long-time friend of John Steinbeck, Bruce Ariss, provided the original sketches of life on the Row during the sardine days. These range from "Fish Cutters," to "Flora's Girls" and "About Ed Ricketts," to name just a few.

In 1988 Bruce Ariss published *Inside Cannery Row: Sketches From The Steinbeck Era.* The cover of that book is a photograph of a mural by Bruce Ariss. The original mural is

Photo: Bob Brueggeman. Inside Ed Ricketts' lab.

now in the Monterey Bay Aquarium. After Bruce Ariss' death in 1994 at the age of 82, the City of Monterey renamed the unfinished extension of Irving Avenue, across from Ricketts' lab, Bruce Ariss Way. Here history buffs can peer through the windows of the three furnished cannery worker cottages depicting how the Spanish, Japanese and Filipino workers lived. More history can be found in the small Steinbeck museum in the back of the former Wing Chong's Market store now containing Alicia's Antiques. The museum was begun by Alicia in 1982 and is open to the public. She is a close friend of Virginia Scardigli, who back in the 1930s and 1940s was one of the group of friends meeting at Ed Ricketts' Lab on the Row.

Cannery Row is also the location of the Monterey Bay National Marine Sanctuary administrative office. The Sanctuary, designated in 1992, is the nation's largest sanctuary, covering about 5,300 square miles of ocean and stretching along California's coastline from the Marin Headlands to Cambria in San Luis Obispo County. It extends from the high tide line to as far as 53 miles offshore. Among its features are the 10,000 foot deep Monterey Canyon, 25 federal and state-

Photo: Pat Hathaway. Fishing nets.

listed rare or endangered species and the largest expanse of kelp beds in the nation. Research and education taking place in the Sanctuary contributes to global efforts to better understand and preserve the marine environment. Since it is designed as a multi-use area, it also allows commercial and recreational fishing and all types of recreational activities.

Prescott Avenue leads up a steep hill from Cannery Row to Highway 68. That area may very well have been the forested hillside overlooking Monterey where the actual paisanos lived who were the models for the paisanos in *Tortilla Flat* (1935), the book that first made John Steinbeck famous. In 1972, Steve Crouch in *Steinbeck Country* after describing some of the changes that had occurred in Monterey since Steinbeck's time and pondering how Steinbeck would have felt about them, wrote the following words, words that still ring true today:

Photo: Rita Costa-Hollmann. Pelicans resting.

"Steinbeck saddened? No, he would have cursed it fervently with mighty, unprintable oaths, turned his back upon it forever, and climbed the steep hills to share a stolen jug of wine with Danny and Pilon, and Jesus Maria Corcoran, the paisanos of his fertile brain, to drink away the ugly memory in that lovely and peaceable place that existed in his mind's eye, Tortilla Flat."

Steve Crouch

Photo: Loran A. List. Cartoonists Eldon Dedini and Gus Ariola at work inside Ricketts' lab.

Photo: David J. Gubernick. Playful pinnipeds.

FORT ORD

I n *Sweet Thursday* (1954), Mack, after a wild goose chase in search of uranium, returns to Monterey "on a flatcar, under a tarpaulin that covered a medium-sized tank destined for Fort Ord." Since before World War II, Fort Ord with its nearly 28,000 acres, had been one of the largest military reservations in the United States. In January 1991 the Secretary of Defense announced Fort Ord's proposed closure. The Fort Ord Reuse Authority (FORA) was established in 1994. FORA's three stated objectives for the Base Reuse Plan are economic development, education research and environmental protection.

The achieved objectives include the establishment of the California State University at Monterey Bay campus in 1995, and the transfer of Fritzsche Airfield to the City of Marina for a commercial airport also in 1995. In 1996, military golf courses were transferred to the City of Marina and undeveloped land transferred to the Bureau of Land Management. Land was also transferred to the University of California for the Monterey Bay Education Science and Technology Center. The Army retained about 3% of the area for the Presidio of Monterey Bay Annex.

Driving through parts of Fort Ord today is much like driving through a ghost town. The troops are gone, the streets are empty; yet boarded up barracks are reminders of a different era. The only noise is due to an occasional passing police patrol car. There are however, miles of bicycle and equestrian trails winding through the thousands of acres within Ford Ord public lands.

On the other hand, on the 1,500 acres acquired by California State University at Monterey Bay, new dormitories and classrooms have been built, although some of the original Fort Ord buildings are still in use. While many of the old cypress trees have been spared, new lawns have been established between buildings throughout the campus.

Straddling the two cities of Marina and Seaside, California State University at Monterey Bay celebrated its opening on August 24, 1995. Academic programs are organized into four centers: 1) Arts, Human Communication, and Creative Technologies; 2) Collaborative Education and Professional Studies; 3) Social and Behavioral Sciences; 4) Science, Technology, and Information Resources. Through these centers' respective institutes, CSUMB offers 13 undergraduate and 3 graduate degree programs, with 2 of the programs administered through CSUMB's university-wide programs. Each of the school's majors or degree programs is organized around a set of major learning outcomes (MLOs) which are stipulated by the faculty in each program.

Photo: Leroy Beal. Miles of paths and trails run through Fort Ord.

Photo: Kira Carrillo Corser. California State University at Monterey Bay.

MOSS LANDING AND ELKHORN SLOUGH

Photo: Rita Costa-Hollmann. An aerial view of Moss Landing with two marine research institutes as well as a mix of commerical and fishing activities.

Before it was diverted by farmers in 1908 away from the mouth of Elkhorn Slough, the Salinas River (the river that John Steinbeck described so aptly in *East of Eden* (1952) as "not a fine river at all, but it was all we had and so we boasted about it") flowed into the Pacific Ocean near Moss Landing. Moss Landing was named after Captain Charles Moss, who established shipping facilities and a pier to develop commercial water traffic from the area in the mid 1800s. Today, harboring two marine research and education institutions, Moss Landing is a center for marine research. Moss Landing Marine Laboratories and Monterey Bay Aquarium Research

Institute both have large research ships based in the harbor. Moss Landing Marine Laboratories (MLML) is the departmental field station for a consortium of six California State University campuses: Fresno, Hayward, Sacramento, San Jose, San Francisco, and Stanislaus. The MLML mission is to: "Provision the Pioneers of the Future."

In September 1997, to replace the old facility of the Moss Landing Marine Laboratories that had been destroyed by the 1989 Loma Prieta earthquake, new ground was broken south of the Moss Landing Harbor. The old site across the one lane bridge on the "island" was not geologically stable enough for rebuilding.

To the east of the laboratories is Elkhorn Slough, one of the largest, relatively undisturbed coastal wetlands remaining in California. The main channel of the slough winds inland nearly seven miles and encompasses over 2,500 acres of marsh and tidal flats. The Elkhorn Slough National Estuarine Research Reserve, which today encompasses about 1,400 acres on the south and east side of the slough, was established after the passage of the Coastal Zone Management Act of 1972. Previous to that, the land had been devoted to dairy farms. The Reserve encompasses a range of habitats from uplands of oak and grassland, to saltmarsh, tidal mudflat and open water. It is managed by the California Department of Fish and Game in cooperation with the National Oceanic and Atmospheric Administration. Additional program support is provided by the Elkhorn Slough Foundation, a non-profit membership-supported organization.

Ongoing programs at the Reserve include water quality monitoring, weather monitoring, annual census of Great Blue Heron and Great Egret breeding colonies and oak woodland restoration. The Reserve also offers workshops for teachers to help them become proficient environmental educators and lead successful field trips for their students on the Reserve.

The Reserve is open to the public and is a paradise for birders. Some 260 species of birds have been identified. Morning and evening fog often blankets the Reserve. On weekends, volunteer docents with scopes lead informative hikes. On a recent hike, the small group I joined observed several red-tailed hawks in the grassland, acorn woodpeckers busy in the woodland and several Great Egrets reflected in the still dark water, to name just a few. Afterwards, the new exhibits at the Visitor Center hands-on museum afforded a unique view into the unseen world of Elkhorn Slough. A huge column of mud, 9-times actual size, displays many of the slough's underwater inhabitants. Interactive displays interpret the saltmarsh and uplands that surround the estuary, birds and birding, research and monitoring, as well as human history.

Since 1984, the 700-acre Moss Landing Wildlife Area has also been managed by the California Department of Fish and Game. The Wildlife Area is part of the original Elkhorn Slough wetlands and contains the most significant remaining example of a pristine saltmarsh along the California coast between San Francisco and Morro Bay. When salt production ceased in the area in 1974, it became a foraging and nesting habitat for huge numbers and varied species of water-associated birds, including some endangered species. This in turn has made the Moss Landing Wildlife Area another prime area for birders.

MISSION ACCOMPLISHED

Obeying the strict orders of the wind
a battalion of ashen clouds
rush east over the slough
declare victory over the retreating sun.

Photo: Robert Almeida. The lights of the harbor illuminate the surrounding boats at Moss Landing.

Photo: Richard W. Gadd. A wooden bridge extends out towards a viewing platform in Elkhorn Slough.

Photo: David J. Gubernick. Old Mission San Antonio de Padua was the third California mission, founded in 1771.

The story of the changes that have taken place since Steve Crouch wrote *Steinbeck Country* (1973) would not be complete without adding a chapter on Jolon, the Mission San Antonio de Padua, and the San Antonio Valley, the main setting for John Steinbeck's *To a God Unknown* (1933).

The Mission, an 85-acre in-holding within Fort Hunter Liggett, is located 18 miles southwest of King City in the San Antonio Valley via Jolon Road. Today ranches, many growing wine grapes, still dot the countryside and in the spring of a wet year the lupine, poppies and mustard turn the roadsides into a kaleidoscope of colors.

At one time, before Highway 101 was built, Jolon Road was part of the old stage route through Central California. The community of Jolon, now within Fort Hunter Liggett, was founded in 1855 as a stage stop for miners bound for the Los Burros mines in the Santa Lucia Mountains. It later developed into the center of commercial and social activity in southern Monterey County. Its gradual demise began with the completion of the Southern Pacific Railroad and the subsequent development of the King City area. From the mid 1920s to 1940, what little remained of the town was owned by William Randolph Hearst. Today, all that remains of the old town are the preserved ruins of the Dutton Hotel, once the old stage stop in Jolon, placed on the National

Photo: Robert Ellis. A hand-made ladder leans against the thick adobe walls of Mission San Antonio.

Register of Historic Places in 1971 and the original structure of the Tidball Store, placed on the National Register in 1976.

The Old Mission San Antonio de Padua was founded by Franciscan padre Friar Junípero Serra, in 1771. It was the third mission established in California and functioned until secularization in 1834. After that it began to fall into a state of neglect and although the U.S. Land Commission formally returned 33 acres of Mission Lands to the Franciscans in 1862, the Mission was abandoned in 1883 and fell into ruins. Almost half a century later, in 1928, the Franciscans returned and began to rebuild the Mission as a training school for brothers of the order. In 1949, the Franciscans were able to repurchase another 46 acres declared surplus by the government. Today, while no longer a training school, it is an active Catholic Parish with the parishioners working together to help the Friars. The museum and grounds give insights into life in the mission days.

* * *

The area around the Mission has seen many changes. The nearby Milpitas Ranch, at one time owned by the Atherton family, was purchased by William Randolph Hearst in 1925 and became part of his extensive holdings reaching inland from San Simeon. He asked Julia Morgan (the architect of the Hearst Castle) to build a hunting lodge for his guests on a hill within a quarter of a mile of the Mission. She completed the large reinforced concrete Mission-style Hacienda in 1936. At the same time he asked her to build a road and bridges for horseback riders across the mountains to connect San Simeon to the San Antonio Valley. However, many of Hearst's Hollywood friends and other luminaries, preferred the longer, easier ride by car to the horseback ride, while others were flown in to the Hacienda. Guests slept in the beautifully appointed rooms, were served meals in the palatial dining room and often spent evenings dancing in the domed ballroom.

Photo: Mary Wurtz. Original mission art.

In December of 1940, William Randolph Hearst sold approximately 158,000 acres of the Milpitas Ranch including the town of Jolon to the Federal Government. Sixteen other landowners also sold their holdings and the area became Fort Hunter Liggett in 1941. The Hacienda was turned into an officers' club.

The Hacienda was placed on the National Register of Historic Places in 1977. While Fort Hunter Liggett is still owned by the United States Army and is used for reserve training, a government contractor runs the Hacienda as a restaurant, lounge and guest lodge open to the public.

Photo: Robert Ellis. Mission interior.

MISSION SAN ANTONIO

The thick adobe walls hoard
the coolness of the night.
Our footsteps echo in the silence.

Hand hewn steps lead down to vats
no longer filled with sacred wine.
Indian arrowheads lie calmly in their case
as impotent as their erstwhile owners
thrown into the white man's world.

A model of the mission that once was
mutely recalls time past when
Franciscan padres ruled their flock.

From Fort Hunter Liggett the Nacimiento Ferguson Road leads over the crest of the Santa Lucia Mountains. It is a winding, two-lane road snaking through oak and redwood groves, past campgrounds and astounding vistas to the Big Sur coast. When winter storms cause the closure of Highway 1 along the coast, the Nacimiento Ferguson Road remains open. For residents in the Lucia and Gorda areas it is then the only means of reaching the outside world.

To a God Unknown (1933) was John Steinbeck's second novel. It is a novel that flows like a river with his vivid descriptions of the San Antonio Valley. He had explored the valley during the summer of 1917, the summer his mother took him to a ranch near Jolon to help him recover from the pleural pneumonia that had almost killed him. While Steinbeck changed the name

Photo: Robert Ellis. An archway inside Mission San Antonio reflecting the Spanish-Mexican heritage.

of the valley to Nuestra Señora, anyone familiar with the area soon recognizes it as the San Antonio Valley. Of course he moved a few landmarks around, but then that's an author's privilege. While there are probably fewer large old live oaks today than there were in Steinbeck's time, the area still remains very much as he described it. The leaves of the trees sway with the rhythm of the wind, the river banks are dense with vegetation, ancient game trails can still be found, and canary mustard stands tall in the spring,

Fountains of flowers
flow over the field.
Rain works miracles.

Photo: Susan Hovermale. Old mission door.

SALINAS VALLEY

"When the rains stop in the spring, the hills along both sides of the Salinas Valley are ablaze with wildflowers: poppies, phacelias, myriad kinds of lupines, and all the other glories native to this place."

Steve Crouch
Steinbeck Country (1973)

Cradled between the arms of the Gabilan and Santa Lucia Mountain ranges, the Salinas Valley is 85 miles long, extending from San Ardo in the south to Monterey Bay in the north. It is a rich, flat valley fashioned eons ago by the waters of the Salinas River flowing both above ground and underground. Those waters, combined with fertile soil and a superb climate, have made the Salinas Valley an agricultural mecca, producing wine grapes, fruits, vegetables and floral products with an estimated value of more than $2 billion annually. Production of organic products, is continually expanding, and accounts for more than 1% of the county's total agricultural value.

For many people, not only in California, but all over the world, the mention of the Salinas Valley immediately brings to mind California Nobel Prize winning author, John Steinbeck. A native of Salinas, as a boy Steinbeck not only roamed the Salinas area, but spent summers with his maternal grandparents at the Hamilton Ranch south of King City. Later, in *Of Mice and Men* (1937), *East of Eden* (1952) and *The Long Valley* (1938), his magnificent descriptions immortalized the Salinas Valley he knew so well. Jackson Benson, John Steinbeck's official biographer, believes that the ranch described in *The Red Pony* was modeled on the Hamilton Ranch.

ABOVE - Photo: Judy Larimore. Picturesque farmlands are a major feature of the Salinas Valley.

PAGE 96-97 - Photo: David J. Gubernick. A tractor sits in a parsley field as the sun sets over this bustling valley.

of her fellow students including one of the Hamilton boys. She recalled the wild horses that used to come down from the "big hill" at the end of Wildhorse Canyon to drink from the river and stated that their tracks can still be seen today.

Much of the history of Monterey County has been preserved in the Monterey County Agricultural and Rural Life Museum located in King City's San Lorenzo Park. Created in 1978 by the County in conjunction with a nonprofit corporation, the well organized and highly informative museum complex relates the story of Monterey County's heritage from mission times to today's advanced agricultural technology. Outside the main museum building, the complex includes a number of other structures. Among these are the King City Depot, a History of Irrigation Museum and a working blacksmith's shop, perhaps modeled on that of Sam Hamilton, and the one room La Gloria School moved from Gonzales. Steinbeck's mother had taught in a one room schoolhouse like this near King City before her marriage.

The Spreckels House, built in 1897 and originally located on the Spreckels Sugar Company Ranch Number One, was moved to the complex in 1980. John Steinbeck may well have been a visitor to a house like this, for, as a young man, during vacations

Photo: Robert Nielsen. Train Station—a part of the Rural Life Museum in King City's San Lorenzo Park.

When the Hamiltons homesteaded their ranch in the 1870s, the 1,600 acres the family acquired was barren and dry. In order to make ends meet Sam Hamilton worked as a blacksmith repairing farm machinery for his neighbors. Today the hills are still dry and used for cattle grazing, but the lowlands are devoted to viticulture, one of the fastest growing agricultural sectors in the area. An elderly neighbor, living on nearby Wildhorse Road, remembers riding to school in King City on horseback as did many

Photo: Kira Carrillo Corser. Strawberries are one of the many regional crops.

Photo: Susan Hovermale. In 1982, the Spreckels Sugar Company ceased production at what was once the world's largest sugar beet operation.

Photo: Susan Hovermale. The old sugar beet refinery stands as a reminder of past glories. Many of the buildings have now been demolished.

ABOVE - Photo: Steve G. Shapiro. A spinach field in Spreckels.

he worked for the Spreckels Company both on the farm and in the processing crew at the plant. At one time Spreckels owned or leased ranches from below King City in the south to Santa Clara in the north. The main business of the ranches was to raise sugar beets. In addition to a small permanent crew at each ranch, Spreckels hired crews of men to maintain the fields throughout the entire ranch system. Many of these were Mexican, Japanese or Filipino. It was from some of these men that Steinbeck heard several of the stories he later used when he wrote *Tortilla Flat* (1935) and *Of Mice and Men* (1937).

The harvested beets were processed at the sugar beet refinery in the company town of Spreckels (located about four miles south of Salinas). In 1898 Claus Spreckels had built the world's largest sugar beet refinery there. In 1982 the Spreckels Sugar Company ceased refinery operations in Spreckels and today Spreckels is no longer a company town.

Since John Steinbeck spent summers at the Hamilton Ranch in the early part of the 20th century, King City has grown tremendously. As a result, new housing developments are invading land formerly devoted to agriculture. King City is not unique in this respect. Most of the other communities in the Salinas Valley are also converting adjoining agricultural acreage to housing tracts.

PROGRESS

Shivering crops mowed down
verdant earth scraped bare
entombed by concrete
a brown skeleton rises
waiting to be fleshed out.
A black dog wanders through
   the gaping maze
sniffing, leaving his mark.

Persistent, raucous hammering drowns
the sunrise bird symphony.
Work progresses
the shell encased,
soon the structure will be complete,
   occupied.
The builder will count his profit,
the bank add another loan to its
   portfolio,
the earth will sigh with grief.

ABOVE - Photo: Robert Nielsen. Rural life in the Salinas Valley.
LEFT - Photo: Gregory Weeks. A colorful shed in Chualar.

Photo: Gale Wrausmann. Fertile fields produce fruit and vegetables for this region.

Photo: Gregory Weeks. Many older family homes fall into disrepair after agricultural interests are sold to major corporate growers and the houses are no longer needed.

Photo: Gale Wrausmann. Dogs get a free hay ride.

North of King City, on both sides of Highway 101, the acres of fields devoted to vegetables are being crowded out by acres of wine grapes. Eucalyptus trees, formerly used as windbreaks, have been cut down to gray hulks in order to increase acreage for planting. Although much of the land has been converted to the planting and growing of wine grapes, the Arroyo Seco area west of the town of Greenfield, remains relatively unchanged. Greenfield has plans to build the Yanks Air Museum on a 440-acre site once known as the "Bill Hansen Ranch." The museum will house a collection of 45 World War II planes and include a movie theater that will show visitors a glimpse of the technological advances that took place during the years of World War II.

The area by the Salinas River to which Lenny and George come when they leave the highway in John Steinbeck's *Of Mice and* Men (1937) lies just a few miles north of Greenfield, east of Highway 101 and south of Soledad. In years of ample rainfall, the river runs deep. The banks are sandy, the willows line the valley side of the river and the debris of the winter's flooding is spread at their base. The paths leading to the river are bordered by dense, high reeds and knee-high wild grasses. As in Steinbeck's time, it still is an area where a man like Lenny might easily remain hidden.

Mission Nuestra Señora de la Soledad, the 13th in the chain of 21 California missions, lies to the west of Highway 101 in Soledad. With the help of volunteers and contributions it is gradually being restored. A good time to visit the mission is during the June Barbecue or the Fall Fiesta.

There is a distinct difference between the climate of the northern and southern Salinas Valley. The southern King City area is considerably warmer than the northern Salinas area. As a result, the southern area grows more warm season crops such as tomatoes. In the north, the high marine morning fog coming in from Monterey Bay generally does not lift till 10 a.m. and returns by 3 p.m., making for much cooler days. The main crops grown are lettuce and broccoli around Salinas and artichokes and brussels sprouts around Castroville.

Photo: Kira Carrillo Corser. Much of the harvesting work is still done by hand as it was done in Steinbeck's day.

Photo: Leroy Beal. An old broken farm wagon deteriorated beyond the point of repair.

ABOVE - Photo: Robert Nielsen. Nature seeks to reclaim its own from man's abandoned handiwork.

LEFT - Photo: David J. Gubernick. Heading west from the Salinas Valley you wind your way towards Carmel Valley via Arroyo Seco (Dry Creek). In the winter and spring months, this creek is far from dry.

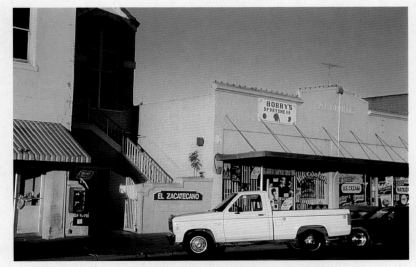

Photo: David J. Gubernick. Downtown Soledad.

commercially in the United States are grown in California.) In *The True Adventures of John Steinbeck, Writer* (1984), Jackson Benson mentions that in the winter and spring of 1921-1922 Steinbeck worked as a laborer with a dredging crew, cutting a

Photo: Mary Wurtz. The predominant crop grown in Castroville, the artichoke capital of the world.

In the early part of the 20th century, before widespread irrigation, the main crops of the Salinas area were potatoes, wheat and sugar beets. Not until the 1920s did vegetables become the predominant crop. In Steinbeck's *East of Eden* (1952), the fictional Adam Trask was one of the pioneers in promoting Salinas Valley lettuce. Today, the Salinas Valley is known as "The Salad Bowl of the World," producing more lettuce varieties than any other county in the United States, with lettuce and broccoli being the two main crops. The two largest agribusinesses are Dole and Tanimura & Antle. Tanimura & Antle began in 1982 when the five local Tanimura brothers joined with Bob Antle and his two sons. (The Antles are an old Salinas family.) They grow, pack and distribute the crops they raise on over 30,000 acres of farmland. They farm from April to November in the Salinas area, then go to the desert area near Yuma, Arizona to farm in the winter, leaving the Salinas area land dormant until Spring. In their highly mechanized and computerized packing plant, near Salinas, they have pioneered the bagged salads that have become popular.

The area near the town of Castroville is devoted to the growth of artichokes and produces about two thirds of California's total artichoke crop. (One hundred percent of all artichokes grown

slough from Salinas to Castroville. He used some of that experience for the setting of his story "Johnny Bear." Today Castroville, with a population of more than 5,000, proclaims itself the "The Artichoke Center of the World," and celebrates with an annual Artichoke Festival every year.

Sufficient water for irrigation of agricultural land has become a problem, especially in the northern Salinas Valley.

Photo: Heidi McGurrin. Farm workers harvest broccoli.

LEFT - Photo: Gregory Weeks. Hay bales arranged neatly in a field.

last twenty years, wine grapes have also become an important crop in the central and northern part. The grapes flourish in the well drained, sandy soil of the bench lands with their warm days, cool nights and fresh breezes from Monterey Bay. Wine grapes are now the fifth largest crop in Monterey County, with nearly 40,000 acres planted in varietal wine grapes. There are numerous wineries, annual Winemakers' Celebrations in late August, as well as "The Great Wine Escape Weekend" in November with many local participating wineries.

Photo: Pat Hathaway. Grapes and wineries flourish on Salinas Valley soils.

ABOVE - Photo: Pat Hathaway. Modern methods are employed in wine production.

RIGHT - Photo: Judy Larimore. Traditional farm in the Salinas Valley.

As a result of pumping the upper aquifers dry, the wells have been sunk deeper and deeper into the aquifers. This has caused salt water from Monterey Bay (now underlying an estimated 22,000 acres in northern Monterey County) to encroach into the wells. In addition, there is a problem with excessive nitrate concentrations. A possible solution is increased usage of drip irrigation, which conserves water and can represent 60% savings in usage. However, at present, drip irrigation does not yet appear to be in general use.

As in the southern Salinas Valley, in the course of the

SALINAS

S ince Steve Crouch's *Steinbeck Country* was published in 1972, the City of Salinas has probably undergone more change and grown more rapidly than any other area of Steinbeck Country. When John Steinbeck was born there in 1902 the town had a population of less than 3,000. In 1970 Salinas had a population of 59,000 which then more than doubled in the subsequent 25 years.

In 1972, the Monterey County Historical Society acquired the Boronda Adobe, built during the Mexican colonial period.

The building was completely restored and dedicated as a museum in 1976. It is both a California Historical Landmark and listed in the National Register of Historical Places. The two buildings next to the Adobe, in the five acre Boronda Adobe Historical Park are a vintage school house and a house designed by noted architect, William H. Weeks.

The Steinbeck House at 132 Central Ave., Steinbeck birthplace and boyhood home, was purchased in 1973 by the Valley Guild, a group of civic-minded, enthusiastic women, who converted the first floor into a gourmet luncheon restaurant. Many family pictures, memorabilia and some furniture donated by the Steinbeck family are on display in the restaurant. The Guild is a non-profit, volunteer organization whose purpose is to maintain and preserve the Steinbeck House and create new revenues for charities in the Salinas Valley. They also run the Best Cellar, a gift shop carrying a large selection of Steinbeck books and gift items.

Foremost among the changes has been the building and opening in June, 1998 of the 37,000-square-foot National Steinbeck Center at 1 Main Street in Old Town Salinas. The Center is a multimedia museum honoring Salinas' native son, who won both the Pulitzer and Nobel Prizes. The museum acquaints the visitor with an overview of Steinbeck's life and times and writings as illustrated by excerpts from his books, as well as film, video and audio clips. A number of the explanatory texts are in both Spanish and English. The National Steinbeck Center also includes a temporary exhibit gallery designed to feature ever-changing art and cultural exhibits.

The building of the Center was made possible by both public and private funds. These included contributions from some of the families of the farmers who had felt betrayed by Steinbeck and had denounced him. The National Steinbeck Center can therefore be recognized as the culmination of the change in the feelings of the citizens of Salinas toward John Steinbeck. After the publication of *In Dubious Battle* (1936), *Of Mice and Men* (1937)

ABOVE - Photo: Pat Hathaway. The Steinbeck House was the boyhood home and birthplace of John Steinbeck. The Valley Guild operates a luncheon restaurant and gift shop.

LEFT - Photo: David J. Gubernick. Old Town Salinas has been aided by the construction of the National Steinbeck Center which has helped spur renewed interest and revitalization efforts in the downtown.

Photo: Susan Cruz. Inside the National Steinbeck Center.

and *The Grapes of Wrath* (1939), he had been accused both of being a Communist and an ingrate who refused to share small town values. At one time his books were burned on Main Street in Salinas. The post WWII publication of *East of Eden* (1952), much of which was set in and around Salinas, did nothing to change his local critics' views.

It was primarily after Steinbeck's death in 1968 that these strong feelings slowly began to change. In March of 1969 the Salinas Public Library was renamed the John Steinbeck Library. In 1973 a six foot, five hundred pound bronze statue sculpted by John Fitzwater was donated to the City of Salinas by the Salinas Soroptimist Club and placed outside the library. The John Steinbeck Library's extensive archival collection of original manuscripts, rare editions, correspondence, photographs, taped inter-

views and other memorabilia connected with the author, were transferred to the new National Steinbeck Center.

1980 marked the first year of the annual Salinas Steinbeck Festival. The Project Director was John Gross, who was also the Director of the John Steinbeck Library, the sponsoring organization. The Festival featured panel discussions and lectures by Steinbeck scholars and friends, films adapted from Steinbeck's novels and stories, walking tours of Steinbeck's home town, Salinas and bus tours of Steinbeck Country including Cannery Row. In 1984, Steinbeck Festival V was held in conjunction with the Second International Steinbeck Congress, bringing together the world's leading authorities on novelist John Steinbeck. The Salinas Steinbeck Festival is held in August of every year. In the early 1990s, after John

Photo: John McCleary. The 37,000 square foot National Steinbeck Center, located in Old Town Salinas, is home to a multi-media museum honoring John Steinbeck.

Photo: Robert Nielsen. Sunset and clouds over Steinbeck Country.

number of other events.

The name Steinbeck has also become popular. Among others there are the Steinbeck Apartments, the Steinbeck Country Art Gallery and the ERA Steinbeck Realty. There is, however, the question whether the existence of the National Steinbeck Center will permanently revitalize Salinas' Old Town for it faces strong competition from huge shopping centers with big box stores that have been built in the newer parts of town.

Gross retired, the Steinbeck Center Foundation took over the sponsorship. In 1998 sponsorship was transferred to the National Steinbeck Center.

In 1992 Salinas' Hartnell College and the Western Stage presented the world premiere of *East of Eden* adapted by playwright in residence, Alan Cook and directed by Western Stage managing artistic director, Tom Humphrey. The play, in three parts, is an unforgettable experience for anyone who has the good fortune to see it. It is repeated periodically. Videotaped excerpts from it can now be seen at the National Steinbeck Center.

Future plans of The Steinbeck Center Foundation, who operates the National Steinbeck Center, call for an adjacent Agricultural, Education and History Center. The Center has sparked redevelopment of Old Town Salinas and the opening of a number of new restaurants and stores. To promote local business, Old Town merchants are supporting a weekly Farmers' Market, as well as a

THE RETURN

*My eyes roam over
the poster of John Steinbeck
pen poised over paper
eyes focused on his words.
Sixty years have passed since
that pen wrote of "the eyes of the hungry"
and their "growing wrath."
Salinas, his birthplace,
rejected, vilified him
banned, burned his books.
Do I hear
sardonic laughter
echoing from his grave?*

The adventurous, wanting to avoid busy Highway 101 north of Salinas, can still take the San Juan Grade Road from Salinas to San Juan Bautista and from there drive up to Fremont Peak State Park. In 1936, in order to preserve the site of the first American flag to fly over California, the State of California acquired Fremont Peak and the adjacent 244 acres of land. Fremont Peak State Park is at the end of the eleven-mile, often narrow, hard-surfaced San Juan Canyon Road that winds up through canyons and over ridges studded with oak, pine, and madrone to an elevation of 3,000 feet. On Steinbeck's last visit to Fremont Peak with his dog, Charley, he wrote, "This solitary peak overlooks my whole childhood and youth" *Travels with Charley* (1962). That day marked the end of his visit to the area where he had grown up, an area that he immortalized in his writing.

While the road leading up to it has changed little in decades, an observatory with its amateur world class 30 inch equatorial reflector has been constructed. The main objective of the Fremont Peak Observatory Association (a group of amateur astronomers) is to promote astronomy through public educational and interpretive programs. Throughout the spring and summer on Saturdays, when the moon is not full, the Fremont Peak Observatory is open for public viewing. A short slide presentation is sometimes given in the evening.

On a clear day the view from Fremont Peak of the surrounding countryside and Monterey Bay is still unobstructed. However, at night a problem being faced by the astronomers is the glow from the bright lighting that has recently been added at Soledad State Prison 22 miles south of Fremont Peak. That light pollution interfering with their observations is upsetting many of the amateur astronomers. They state that it is not enough to have clear skies. They must also be dark.

RIGHT - Photo: David J. Gubernick. A bobcat surveys his immediate surroundings. Despite growth pressures on the Central Coast, wildlife remains abundant in the undeveloped hills and valleys.

FREMONT PEAK

Like an ardent suitor
the fog kisses the mountain
caresses it
enfolds it in a gentle embrace

A sudden gust of wind
tears the lovers apart
leaves the bare peak
blushing in the glow
of the setting sun.

PEOPLE

"John Steinbeck's novels reinforce one vision—a majestic landscape with proud heroic people... Steinbeck once described the people as 'whores, pimps, gamblers, and sons of bitches,' as well as 'Saints and angels and martyrs and holy men,' (Cannery Row) by which he meant the same thing."

ABOVE - Photo: Lucy Ash. Scuba divers preparing to dive into Monterey Bay.

TOP RIGHT - Photo: Lucy Ash. Tidepools hold a particular fascination for children.

BOTTOM RIGHT - Photo: Robert Nielsen. Workers are busy harvesting celery.

Photo: Heidi McGurrin. A laborer glances up from his hard work in fields of broccoli.

Photo: Helene Constant. Peter Worden rests near an old Spanish house. He ran the well-known "OZ" restaurant on Cannery Row in the 1950s.

Photo: Heidi McGurrin. The children of trajabadores (workers) *at play in Soledad.*

ABOVE - Photo: Debi Szarkowski Effron. Local cowboys gather after a calf branding at a ranch in Carmel Valley.

LEFT - Photo: Heidi McGurrin. Local characters: Chocolate, Ray Hackworth and Roosevelt Johnson.

LEFT TOP - Photo: Kira Carrillo Corser. School children with jump ropes in Monterey.

BOTTOM LEFT - Photo: Helene Constant. Fred Nason, a member of the Esselen tribe at the Ceremonial Grounds.

BOTTOM RIGHT - Photo: Kira Carrillo Corser. Rodolfo Tapia Salazar of San Ardo, pictured here with his son Alexis, is a neighborhood hero. He teaches kids boxing and takes them hiking as an alternative to gangs.